www.TimeMasteryLab.com

PRAISE FOR *STREET-SMART STRATEGIES FOR TIME MASTERY*

I recommend this book to all law students and legal practitioners. The book addresses time management skills in a useful and focussed manner. This book is a must-have in the library of all professionals.

– **Mr. Baiross**
   Advocate & Solicitor and Managing Partner,
   IRB Law LLP

The ability to manage time well is such an important life skill for everyone, especially a working mother who has to manage family commitments and a demanding career at the same time. This book offers very practical tips on how to achieve it effectively.

– **Ms. Jomay Wan**
   Former Senior Vice President, MediaCorp Pte Ltd

Street-Smart Strategies for Time Mastery is a must-read for anyone battling procrastination. Read this book now and learn from the time masters.

– **Ms. Choo Li Lin**
  Applied Linguist and Educator

I highly recommend this book for people of all ages who are living in the highly competitive and time-pressured world that is the 21st century. Amazingly concise yet spot-on with lots of pearls of wisdom, the authors waste no time with unnecessary information overload, and present the readers with nuggets of wisdom which are both easy to understand and to implement. As a time-pressured mother-of-two juggling full-time work as a dermatologist and dermatologic surgeon, this book has been invaluable in giving me tips to be a better master of my time!

– **Dr. Angeline Yong**
  Dermatologist, Angeline Yong Dermatology

Drs. Kumaran Rajaram and Eugene Tan have written a must-read book for all who wish for more than 24 hours a day. Read this book and learn the secrets of time mastery from the two super achievers!

– **Dr. Kong Jing Wen**
  Consultant Family Physician

As a full-time working professional who is faced with frequent tests and exams in my job, whilst trying to juggle family, relationship, and religion commitments, I find myself feeling at my wits' end at times. It was not until I read this book that I realised I was struggling with the time traps illustrated here! I had also never done a personal time audit until this book inspired me to do so. Learning about the 6 strategies for time mastery has benefited me immensely, and the advice from this book has propelled me to change my habits so that I am no longer a "slave" to my commitments. Instead, I learned to be a "master" at crafting time out for myself. Now, I feel more invigorated to study, work, yet still find quality time for my loved ones and family! As the book aptly says, "Do the right things first and do them fast." I recommend anyone to read this book as one of the first right things to do now!

– **Dr. Sophie Cai**
  Dermatology Senior Resident

A simple and practical formula that one can easily implement to achieve greater effectiveness in life! An excellent read, especially for young learners who wish to work smarter and accomplish more in less time!

– **Dr. Liu Yuchun**
  Scientist

This book provides pragmatic and achievable tips to everyone who has experienced challenges in time management and organisation, with the diverse experiences of the two successful authors serving as a precedent for many students. The strategies in this book are practical and applying them would enable one to maximise time and productivity. A recommended read for anyone in need of a reminder that they can be masters of their own time.

– **Ms. Ong Rui Xiu Clarice**
  Undergraduate, Accountancy and Business

This book is a refreshing read and has a crystal-clear goal of helping its readers such as myself make full use of our limited time in the day. This can be done by eliminating distractions, prioritising urgent and vital items, and doing tasks immediately without distractions. I really love the distilled recommendations this book provides, along with established evidence, which allows me to quickly decide on my next steps to better manage my time.

– **Mr. Koon Soon Lee**
  Undergraduate, Accountancy and Business

Personally, as a driven and ambitious student, I have always looked up to industry heavyweights such as Jamie Dimon (CEO of JPMorgan Chase) and Ruth Porat (CFO of Google). They have the same 24 hours as we do, yet seem to be able to accomplish so much more. Perhaps intellect plays a part, but based on the interviews they have done, a common ingredient to success that they cited is disciplined time management. This book is an easily digestible piece which compels us to sit down and analyse the way we utilise our time to make it more efficient and productive. Useful templates such as the "Personal Time Audit" also help us to plan our time better, and the book is suitable for both student and adult learners who want to achieve more in the same amount of time.

– **Ms. Lau Shu Qing**
   Undergraduate, Accountancy and Business

An insightful read! This book systematically explores the ways in which time is "stolen" from us and enlightens us with practical tips on how to save time. It is easy to comprehend and the suggested methods are simple to apply. A must-have for anyone who wishes to excel in life.

– **Dr. Chung Pin Soon**
   Family Physician

Dr. Kumaran Rajaram and Dr. Eugene Tan expertly detailed strategies and tips on the long-standing issue of time management. The book provides modern and refreshing perspectives that were highly relatable and bound to leave readers eager for more. The actionable steps outlined to tackle the major "time traps" to help supercharge productivity are simple and concise tools. Yet, there are delicate frameworks catering to the attributes of each individual, providing a robust and holistic approach for creating unique and personalised solutions for time management. Be empowered with this book and help yourself "create" more time, rather than worry about it.

– **Mr. Nicholas Teoh Hong Hok**
   Undergraduate, Accountancy and Business

Dr. Kumaran Rajaram and Dr. Eugene Tan deliver with absolute clarity a set of time-management principles that dispel any doubt of how they are able to achieve so much every day. The brevity of the book reflects at once the core of the book—to invite wisdom through focus.

– **Mr. Raphael Yee**
   Undergraduate, Philosophy and Computer Science

STREET-SMART STRATEGIES *for* TIME MASTERY

DR EUGENE ST TAN · DR KUMARAN RAJARAM

Candid Creation Publishing

First published April 2020

Candid Creation Publishing books are available through most major bookstores in Singapore. For bulk order of our books at special quantity discounts, please email us at enquiry@candidcreation.com.

STREET-SMART STRATEGIES FOR TIME MASTERY

Authors	: Dr Eugene ST Tan and Dr Kumaran Rajaram
Publisher	: Phoon Kok Hwa
Editor	: Tansey Tang
Cover designer	: Ryanne Ng
Layout	: Corrine Teng
Published by	: Candid Creation Publishing LLP
	167 Jalan Bukit Merah
	#05-12 Connection One Tower 4
	Singapore 150167
Website	: www.candidcreation.com
Facebook	: www.facebook.com/CandidCreationPublishing
Email	: enquiry@candidcreation.com

National Library Board, Singapore Cataloguing-in-Publication Data

Name: Tan, Eugene Sern Ting. | Rajaram, Kumaran, 1976- author.

Title: Street-smart strategies for time mastery / Dr Eugene ST Tan, Dr Kumaran Rajaram.

Description: Singapore : Candid Creation Publishing, 2020.

Identifier(s): OCN 1144086869 | ISBN 978-981-14-5117-1 (paperback)

Subject(s): LCSH: Time management. | Life skills.

Classification: DDC 640.43--dc23

CONTENTS

ACKNOWLEDGEMENTS

We sincerely express our heartfelt appreciation to the following people who have contributed to the successful publication of this book:

Our spouses and families for their unwavering support and encouragement;

All the other people who have contributed to this book in one way or another.

FOREWORD

This book is very useful not only for students and adult learners who are daunted by pressing demands on their time but also for those who want to make better use of their time. Good time management is a skill that is relevant to students and will only become increasingly essential as students transit into young working professionals when they embark on their careers.

Developing good working habits early will ensure students start off on the right foot. Change is always harder when old habits have become entrenched. To this end, the authors provide insightful and actionable suggestions on how students can assess whether they are managing their time well and what they can do to better manage their time. The authors have made available valuable toolkits in their book that will serve as an impetus to students who desire to spend their time wisely and fruitfully to act now. Strange as it may sound initially, there is always time only if you know where to look for it and what to do with it, and practice makes perfect.

Associate Professor Low Kin Yew
Associate Dean (Undergraduate Academic)
Nanyang Business School,
Nanyang Technological University

PREFACE

It is fascinating to live in a world where change is the only constant. In today's rapidly evolving environment, students and adult learners are expected to fulfil multiple tasks and do them well. In order for them to manage these expectations and challenges, they must be competent in certain skill sets.

One of the key competencies in achieving success in life is the art of mastering what you do with your time, commonly referred to as "time management". It is a convenient term to use even for this book, but it is important to keep in mind that time management is actually a misnomer because time cannot be manipulated. As we are going to see in the subsequent pages, time management is actually all about personal mastery.

Until the day when time travel becomes a reality, no one in this world has the capability to alter time. In a single day, each of us has a fixed amount of time, equivalent to 24 hours or 1,440 minutes in a day, or more precisely, 86,400 seconds in a day. The clock is continually ticking away even as you are reading this. Despite an ample amount of time being at our disposal per day, we often hear people complaining that they are unable to complete their daily tasks.

When we set out to write this book for students and adult learners, we had only one clear purpose in mind: to help you to effectively manage your time, and attain your desired goals as you have planned. As you read the chapters in this book, we hope that you will reflect on the salient time mastery principles and strategies that resonate with your beliefs and personal circumstances, and actively implement one or more of these ideas in your life. When you take concrete, practical actions to improve the way you use your time, you will create more time to do the things you value and enjoy, and ultimately achieve greater success and happiness in your life.

PART *one*

IN SEARCH OF TIME

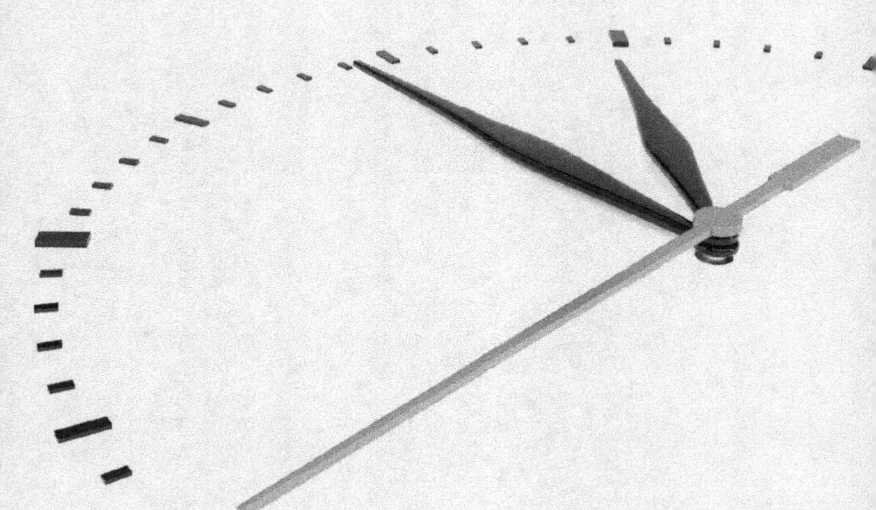

IS THERE ENOUGH TIME?

"If you want to make good use of your time,
you've got to know what's most important,
and then give it all you've got."

- Lee Iacocca,
former President of
Ford Motor Company and Chrysler Corporation

 ## THE SECRET TO ACHIEVING MORE

Let's face it. The typical student in Singapore has to cope with an incredibly heavy workload. The day is usually reserved for attending school. After school, there may be co-curricular activities or meetings. This is followed by homework and preparation for tests or exams, as well as preparation for projects and presentations. For many students, there may be extra tuition and enrichment classes. On top of that, there are family commitments, social life, and relationships. It is also an uphill battle to resist the incessant allure of Facebook, Instagram, YouTube, email, and instant messaging apps, all of which are a click away. Akin to school students, adult learners face very similar challenges, particularly if they have to study part-time on top of managing a busy full-time job. Is it possible at all to find enough time for all these activities?

Over the years, a great deal has been written about time management. There are books that promise to teach you how to gain an extra hour every day, or an extra couple of hours, or even how to double your 24 hours! The reality is, each of us only has 24 hours a day, so why is it that some people can do so much within that 24 hours, while others lament that they don't have enough time for all their tasks?

THE SECRET LIES IN HOW YOU MAKE FULL USE OF YOUR 24 HOURS TO ACHIEVE THE GOALS YOU SET.

The secret lies in how you make full use of your 24 hours to achieve the goals you set. And we're not just talking about the small figure of 24 hours. There is much more at stake—168 hours in a week, 720 hours in a month, and 8,760 hours in a year. If you learn the strategies in this book to master all this time that is available to you, you will find that it is possible to do so much more.

OUR PERSONAL JOURNEYS IN TIME MASTERY

"Your visions will become clear only when you can look into your own heart. Who looks outside, dreams; who looks inside, awakes."

**- Carl Jung,
founder of analytical psychology**

DR. KUMARAN RAJARAM: HOW I GOVERNED THE CLOCK IN MY PURSUIT OF TIME MASTERY

During my younger days, my circumstances made me realise and embrace the importance of managing time effectively as I had to learn to competently deal with varying priorities concurrently. Rising to the highest pinnacle by achieving an academic qualification of

Ph.D. with Distinction (outstanding achievement) and becoming a professor in a globally reputed university were achievements that were possible only through a high level of commitment, crystal-clear focus, determination to overcome compelling challenges, and strict discipline with effective time management. I have had the opportunity to experience the life of an adult learner, and later in my career have taught adult learners. This is to say I had to literally work, manage my personal and family commitments, and study at the same time, by catering time to prepare for my lessons, do my assignments, complete project work, study for final exams, and so on. This is on top of ensuring I spent some quality time with my family, and many other commitments and responsibilities. A typical day consisted of spending time at work from morning till around 6 p.m. On class days, I had to go straight from work to attend lessons till late in the evening. After arriving home on those days, I had to decide how to spend the very little time I had left effectively preparing for the next day's work before I went to bed. This happened three days a week, setting aside the weekends. At times, there would also be weekend classes that I needed to attend.

As such, reality has taught me to plan my time effectively. I had to ensure I balanced my time well so that I could cope with my highly demanding studies, have adequate rest so that I could perform competently at work, spend quality time with my family, and build my relationships with my then girlfriend, now wife, and close friends and relatives. Moreover, I was an active soccer player, marathon runner, and social volunteer, who enjoyed reading, listening to music, and appreciating nature. Despite my busy schedule, I have never failed to be actively involved in what I love to do outside my work and studies, which makes me an all-rounder.

Currently, effective time management is even more crucial as I have to balance my varying roles and responsibilities as a professor and a practising consultant with the industry, while volunteering in community-related works as well as maintaining a quality family life and being a sport enthusiast. The mantra is to be highly disciplined and committed to the day-to-day activities, not procrastinating on tasks that need to be done, being able to clearly prioritise by differentiating the tasks that are important versus urgent, and acting on those diligently in accordance. Through my years of experience, I have learned that personal mastery of time management is not

> **PERSONAL MASTERY OF TIME MANAGEMENT IS NOT AN OPTION BUT RATHER A FUNDAMENTAL REQUIREMENT FOR HAPPINESS AND CAREER SUCCESS.**

an option but rather a fundamental requirement for happiness and career success.

My secret to this is to mindfully plan and allocate time carefully as well as stay highly disciplined to follow those plans as a serious commitment, which I strongly hold as a personal value and principle. I am glad to share this well-tested and proven formula that has enabled me to earn various accolades and achievements in my academic qualifications, work, and personal life.

DR. EUGENE TAN: MY RELENTLESS PURSUIT OF TIME MASTERY

I first became interested in the subject of time management during my student days in Raffles Junior College. I experienced a bit of culture shock when I first entered junior college, as I suddenly became saddled with endless assignments, tests, and after-school activities, and could not find any time for a social life. I was convinced that either I was making mistakes in time management, or there must be a better way to manage my time. I started by asking my friends and classmates how they managed their time and picked up a few useful tips. However, I was far from satisfied, so I went further by researching numerous books written by experts on time management. I ended up with a truckload of ideas and time management "systems", some of which were difficult to implement and not applicable for students. Thereafter, I identified the best ideas and tested them, and in the process, formulated a simple and effective set of strategies for mastering the way I manage my time. I am confident that these ideas will work for you as a student or adult learner, regardless of the level of education you are currently at.

Just to share with you my personal experience, I applied these time mastery strategies while I was a medical student in the National University of Singapore, and the result was immensely satisfying. I was able to find time to study my medical textbooks, yet had enough time to give private tuition to several students, take part in activities such as Toastmasters and Youth Challenge, write a book on dating and relationships, give public talks, write articles for magazines, create and market websites, conduct research and publish articles in medical journals, take on the role of the Editor for a management journal, and so on. The most challenging year was in my final year of medical school where I had to revise all the major subjects studied in the previous years to prepare for my final Bachelor of Medicine, Bachelor of Surgery examination, but that was also the time I accomplished the most in terms of publishing and marketing my book, writing and publishing journal articles, and taking part in various activities outside campus.

Through my transitions into different phases of life, first as a student, then as a young working adult juggling long hours of work with studying for incessant post-graduate tests and exams (during my house officer, medical officer, and registrar years), and currently as a middle-aged dermatologist who is constantly endeavouring to strike a fine balance between the four pillars that comprise my professional work, voluntary activities, personal development, and family commitments, it is interesting to reflect on how I have been managing my time. My ever-expanding to-do list is getting longer and longer each year, to the point that it is no longer feasible to complete everything that I want to do. I figured out that my best bet to achieve my to-do list is to invest time in crystallising my most important goals, take action on the most important and meaningful tasks at any one time, and raise my efficiency as much as possible.

Though my priorities have continually evolved across the years, I have observed that the fundamental principles of time mastery remain the same. Even as technology becomes increasingly interwoven

THOUGH MY PRIORITIES HAVE CONTINUALLY EVOLVED ACROSS THE YEARS, THE FUNDAMENTAL PRINCIPLES OF TIME MASTERY REMAIN THE SAME.

into the world we live in, these time mastery principles have stood and will continue to stand the test of time. As you read the rest of this book, I am excited and truly grateful to have the opportunity to share these ideas with you.

Chapter 3

BEWARE OF THE 3 TIME TRAPS

*"You can't make up for lost time.
You can only do better in the future."*

**- Ashley Ormon,
author of *God in Your Morning***

Time mastery is such an important life skill that we cannot wait to share with you the very best time mastery strategies for students and adult learners. But before we dive into them, let us first look at 3 common "time traps" that steal your precious time and productivity, along with supporting explanations of why it is absolutely crucial for you to avoid them. Basically, time traps are ways that people mismanage their time.

TIME TRAP #1

Multitasking

ACTION STEP

Do one thing and only one thing at a time.

"You can have it all. Just not all at once."

**- Oprah Winfrey,
talk show host and billionaire philantropist**

 ## MULTITASKING: GOOD OR BAD?

If you ask most students and adults whether they multitask at home, chances are, you will probably get a positive response. After all, they believe it helps them to save time. We know of a student who revises for her exams, watches television, eats snacks, surfs the internet, and chats with friends online—all at the same time! At first glance, it may seem like she is accomplishing a lot of things within a limited time span. But the truth is, she is wasting her time on many unnecessary activities and compromising on the effectiveness of her exam preparation.

Although many of us like to multitask in this digital age, research published by Stanford University in 2009 has shown that multitasking slows down our performance in simple tasks, and we may end up spending more time to complete the task than originally required. This applies not just to studying but also to other tasks such as project work. The traffic police know this and are therefore clamping down on drivers who use their mobile phones during driving, because there is robust evidence to show that multitasking slows down our reaction time.

According to neuroscientists, our brains are simply not wired for multitasking. There is however, one piece of research by the University of Utah published in a psychology journal in 2010 that found that 2.5% of college students were able to multitask without impairing their mental performance. These students were labelled as "super-taskers". Unfortunately, such super-taskers are few and far between in real life. Unless you really are a gifted super-tasker or multitasking expert, it is ultimately more productive to focus on one task at a time and avoid multitasking. American motivational guru Brian Tracy calls this the Principle of Single Handling which basically

> **OUR BRAINS ARE SIMPLY NOT WIRED FOR MULTITASKING.**

means to stay on an important task and stick to it until it is completed.

Single-tasking, or the practice of doing only one thing at a time, allows you to devote your entire attention and energy to completing the task. Having a precise focus often leads you to enter a natural state of flow where doing the task with quality and efficiency becomes a breeze. If you finish your key tasks faster, you will have more time to play and relax, and thereby feel less stressed. Starting from today, make it a habit to do only one thing at a time.

TIME TRAP #2

Procrastination

ACTION STEP

Do it now. Just do it.

"Time is really the only capital that any human being has, and the only thing he can't afford to lose."

- Thomas Edison, inventor

 ## THE PROS AND CONS OF PROCRASTINATION

Have you ever procrastinated in your life?

Simply put, procrastination means to put off or delay a task until another time or day. We ourselves are guilty of procrastinating every now and then, and we are rather certain that you will have procrastinated at some point in your life too, even if you have not realised it. If your English essay is due in a week's time, you may put it off until one or two days before the deadline because if there is no sense of urgency, it is just so difficult to sit down for a couple of hours to write out the essay. And it is common to see students doing last minute, intensive "cramming" for examinations, all because they procrastinated instead of starting their revision earlier.

Procrastination is a double-edged sword and it really can be good or bad depending on the situation.

It is good to procrastinate if you have a big plate of deep-fried chicken on the table in front of you, and you hesitate to eat all five pieces because you are worried that it may be detrimental to your health. Whenever the latest model of popular smartphones, such as the Apple iPhone, is newly launched, it is common to see long, snaking queues of people at the sales outlets, all eager to get their hands on the latest gadget as early as possible. In this situation, it may be wise to procrastinate and suppress your desire to purchase the device immediately by differentiating your wants from your needs, because the prices of electronic gadgets will invariably depreciate over time.

> **PROCRASTINATION IS A TERRIBLE ENEMY IN OUR PERSONAL TIME MANAGEMENT.**

However, procrastination is a terrible enemy in our personal time management as it slows us down and wastes a lot of our precious time. If you are the type who is always procrastinating when it comes to studying for exams and ends up spending more time surfing the internet or chatting with friends than doing your revision, you will be highly inefficient in your exam preparation. Consequently, before you even realise it, you may have run out of time to revise all the topics in the syllabus before the day of the exam.

REWIRING YOUR BRAIN TO OVERCOME PROCRASTINATION

If you master the art of overcoming procrastination, it will supercharge your personal efficiency. There are many time management and self-improvement books that explore the many ways that you can overcome procrastination. One of our favourite strategies to beat procrastination is adapted from top American motivational guru Anthony Robbins' method. Essentially, we learnt from him that there are two fundamental forces that drive human behaviour— pain and pleasure. To motivate yourself to take action quickly, you should create thoughts of either increased pain or increased pleasure in your mind, or a combination of both as shown in Figure 3.1. Harnessing these two forces in the correct manner is the key to beating procrastination and taking action.

> **THERE ARE TWO FUNDAMENTAL FORCES THAT DRIVE HUMAN BEHAVIOUR— PAIN AND PLEASURE.**

Figure 3.1   The fundamental forces that drive
human behaviour

Let us take exam preparation as an example. You have an important exam coming up in one month. If you are procrastinating your revision, think about what pain you will feel if you do not prepare well for the exam. The likely outcome is poor grades, and you may become the laughing stock of your classmates. If you fail the exam badly, you may even be held back for a year. Ultimately, it can potentially affect your future career path.

Next, think about what pleasure you will feel if you start studying immediately. You will have more time to prepare for the exam, and you will be less stressed towards the end when other classmates who started revision late may have to burn the midnight oil. If you study well, you are likely to achieve good grades for the exam and you will feel accomplished and satisfied. It is also a stepping stone to a bright future.

Once you have convinced yourself that there is much pain to suffer if you do not start on the task, and much pleasure to derive from starting on the task, your mind will be supercharged to believe that there is only one logical way forward, which is to take action immediately. To quote Nike's famous slogan, "Just do it".

TIME TRAP #3

Majoring in the minor

ACTION STEP

Do what is important first.

"Most of us spend too much time on what is urgent, and not enough time on what is important."

- Stephen Covey, author of
The 7 Habits of Highly Effective People

 ## DO YOU "MAJOR IN THE MINOR"?

Former British Prime Minister Benjamin Disraeli is famous for saying, "Don't major in the minor." That is precisely what some students do. What this means is that they spend an exorbitant amount of time on minor activities that have very little impact, if any, on their success. These activities include chatting with friends, watching television or YouTube videos, mindlessly surfing the internet, and frequently checking Facebook posts and other social media updates.

As a regional technology hub, Singapore is known to be the most wired nation in Southeast Asia. This is clearly reflected in the exponential growth of internet penetration and usage among residents over the past decade. In 2011, *The Straits Times* reported that Singaporeans were the heaviest internet users in Southeast Asia, spending an average of 25 hours online per week. Six years later in 2017, a survey by Ernst & Young with 1,000 respondents revealed that Singapore residents spend an average of 12 hours 42 minutes on their digital devices daily. These devices include mobile phones, tablets, personal computers, laptops, and video game consoles.

Perhaps, what is more alarming are the findings of a worldwide survey of 38,000 children across 29 countries conducted by Digital Quotient Institute in 2017, showing that children in Singapore spend an average of 35 hours per week online, 3 hours more than the global average. Although we do not have the latest figures of internet usage at the time of writing, we would not be surprised if our time spent online has increased further.

DO THE REALLY IMPORTANT THINGS FIRST

So, if you find yourself never having "enough time", it is important to reflect on whether you are spending too much non-essential time on digital devices. Remember, the issue does not lie with the digital devices; rather, it lies in whether we use them in a disciplined and constructive manner.

> THE ISSUE DOES NOT LIE WITH THE DIGITAL DEVICES; RATHER, IT LIES IN WHETHER WE USE THEM IN A DISCIPLINED AND CONSTRUCTIVE MANNER.

Every single day, you must understand your priority, or the most important task that you have to complete that day, in order to move you closer towards your goal. For example, your goal may be to achieve an 'A' grade for a subject's final exam. In this example, your major task may be to revise your notes and textbook, practise exam questions, or reflect on the mistakes you have made in previous tests and assignments. You should then endeavour to spend most of your time working on that major task, and only use your leftover time for minor unimportant tasks. This way, you can truly "major in the major, and minor in the minor".

In our experience, the best way to develop an awareness of how you are spending your time is to do a personal time audit. In the following chapter, we shall share with you how to go about doing one.

Chapter 4

PERSONAL TIME AUDIT

*"It's not enough to be busy; so are the ants.
The question is, what are we busy about?"*

**- Henry David Thoreau,
essayist, poet, and philosopher**

Successful companies and organisations perform audits on a regular basis for various aspects of their work processes, so that they can identify flaws in the current system and find ways to correct these flaws to improve the system. Similarly, the purpose of a personal time audit is to find out how you are currently spending your time so that you can identify time wasters and uncover hidden time in your life. Personally, we found this exercise very useful in helping us realise how much time we have been wasting on various unimportant activities.

 **WEEKLY TIME AUDIT TEMPLATE**

The following is our template for a personal time audit that we have used during our student days. It does not have to be anything fancy, and you should not spend too much time creating it. Let us first go through an example of a student's time audit in Table 4.1, before you start doing your own.

Weekly Activities	Hours in a Week	Comments
Total Hours in 1 Week	168	
Hours for School	30	
Hours for Co-Curricular Activities/Enrichment and Tuition Classes	6	
Hours for Sleep	56	
Hours for Family	14	

Hours for Transport	14
Hours for Meals	14
Hours for Leisure/ Entertainment (leisure internet surfing, social media, movies, videos, phone calls, online chatting, time with friends)	14
Hours for Personal Care (toileting, showering, personal grooming)	7
Hours for Other Activities (gym, sports, reading, pets, emails, housework)	7
Total Hours Spent	162
Free Hours Remaining for High Priority Tasks	6

Table 4.1 Weekly time audit template

In this example, you can see that after accounting for all the activities in the week, this student will have about six free hours left each week for major tasks such as revising for exams. Sounds like too little time, doesn't it?

 **DAILY TIME AUDIT TEMPLATE**

If you find it too much of a stretch to audit your time for an entire week, an easier way is to audit your time for a day first, so that you can calculate the number of free hours you have in a day. An example template is shown in Table 4.2. Thereafter, do the daily audit for a few more days if possible, and extrapolate the results to an entire week.

It is normal for the number of free hours per day to vary from day to day, as your schedule is unlikely to be identical every day. What is more important is to determine the number of free hours per week, because that can be smartly utilised to work on a highly important priority task.

Daily Activities	Hours in a Day	Comments
Total Hours in 1 Day	24	
Hours for School	7	
Hours for Co-Curricular Activities / Enrichment and Tuition Classes	3	
Hours for Sleep	7	
Hours for Family	0.5	
Hours for Transport	1.5	
Hours for Meals	1.5	
Hours for Leisure/ Entertainment (leisure internet surfing, social media, movies, videos, phone calls, online chatting, time with friends)	1.5	
Hours for Personal Care (toileting, showering, personal grooming)	1	

Hours for Other Activities (gym, sports, reading, pets, emails, housework)	0.5
Total Hours Spent	23.5
Free Hours Remaining for High Priority Tasks	0.5

Table 4.2   Daily time audit remplate

To benefit fully from this exercise, stop reading momentarily and take the next 30 minutes to perform your personal weekly or daily time audit.

 ## RECTIFYING THE BIGGEST TIME WASTERS

After you have completed your personal time audit, you should next go through each category, identify the biggest time wasters, and cut down on those in order to free up valuable time and increase the number of free hours you have per week. Table 4.3 shows some common time wasters and suggestions on how you can rectify them.

Common Time Waster	How to Rectify
Excessive Sleeping	Sleep one hour less every day. One strategy is to sleep 30 minutes later and wake up 30 minutes earlier.
Commuting to and from School	Read or listen to educational audio or your voice-recorded notes during commuting. Avoid peak-hour traffic by going to school earlier if possible.
Checking Facebook and Social Media throughout the Day	Schedule fixed time slots to check Facebook posts or update your status, such as during lunchtime and before bedtime.
Watching YouTube, Facebook and Instagram Videos	Decide on a fixed amount of time each week on these activities, and DO NOT exceed the time limit. Better still, schedule them as a reward for completing your major tasks, which will keep you motivated to stay on track.

Table 4.3   Common time wasters and rectification strategies

Now that we have identified the common mistakes made by students and adult learners in managing their time, it is time that you analyse your daily life and see if you are guilty of one or more of these time wasters. Starting from today, be consciously aware of these traps, and avoid them as much as you can. Eliminating time grabbers is an essential prerequisite to successful personal time mastery.

ELIMINATING TIME GRABBERS IS AN ESSENTIAL PREREQUISITE TO SUCCESSFUL PERSONAL TIME MASTERY.

In the following section, you will learn the six street-smart strategies of time mastery along with their accompanying recommended action steps, which will be particularly useful for students and adult learners who are looking to maximise their potential for achievement.

PART two

THE 6 STREET-SMART STRATEGIES FOR TIME MASTERY

Chapter 5

STRATEGY #1:
VISION WITH ACTION

*"Lack of direction, not lack of time, is the problem.
We all have 24-hour days."*

**- Zig Ziglar,
motivational speaker**

Before you can achieve anything in life,
you must know *exactly* what you want
to achieve and take action on it
without any procrastination.

ACTION STEP

Set a precise target and
take immediate action on it.

WHY IS IT IMPORTANT TO HAVE CRYSTAL CLEAR VISION?

What makes an eagle successful in catching its prey? The secret lies in the eagle having a bird's eye view from the sky, from which they can easily zoom in on their targets on land.

What is the common denominator of all successful new businesses? All successful businesses have well-formulated business plans that contain their mission statements, short-term and long-term goals, business development strategies, manpower planning, competition analysis, financial analysis, and marketing and advertising strategies. A good business plan gives an overview of the business and its industry, so that the business knows exactly what to do to succeed.

Similarly, if you want to excel in your studies, it is not enough to tell yourself that you want to do well because that is subjective and vague. For each subject, you should set yourself a precise target and write it down. An example of a precise goal is to achieve an 'A' grade for Chemistry in the final year-end examination. Or perhaps all you need is a 'B+' and above for your final module in the Business course, so that you can secure a GPA of more than 4.0. You must be crystal clear about what you are aiming to achieve for each individual subject, so that you do not waste too much time engaging in non-productive activities.

HIGH ACHIEVEMENT STARTS WITH VI-ACTION

Vi-Action, which is the art of taking action on your vision, is a pre-requisite to peak performance and successful achievements in your studies, work, and personal life. While you might be certain of your goals and targets, the number one enemy to taking action is procrastination. You need to defeat procrastination with all your might; otherwise it is difficult for you to take action on your vision.

Procrastination negatively affects your productivity. It can cause damaging effects, in terms of wasting valuable time, energy, and effort, and can affect both your career and personal milestones or targets. You should avoid procrastination at all costs as the repercussions are highly detrimental to your well-being.

THE K-ACHIEVER MATRIX

The K-Achiever Matrix is an analysis framework that uses two primary variables, namely clarity of vision and procrastination, to determine the performance level of an individual. Clarity of vision refers to the ability to know exactly what you need to do in order to achieve the desired goal. Procrastination refers to the delay in acting on the tasks at hand. This framework enables you to have a quick understanding of where you are right now and how you can take the required actions to move forward in achieving your goals.

Figure 5.1 presents the K-Achiever Matrix framework, with the individual quadrants explained in Table 5.1.

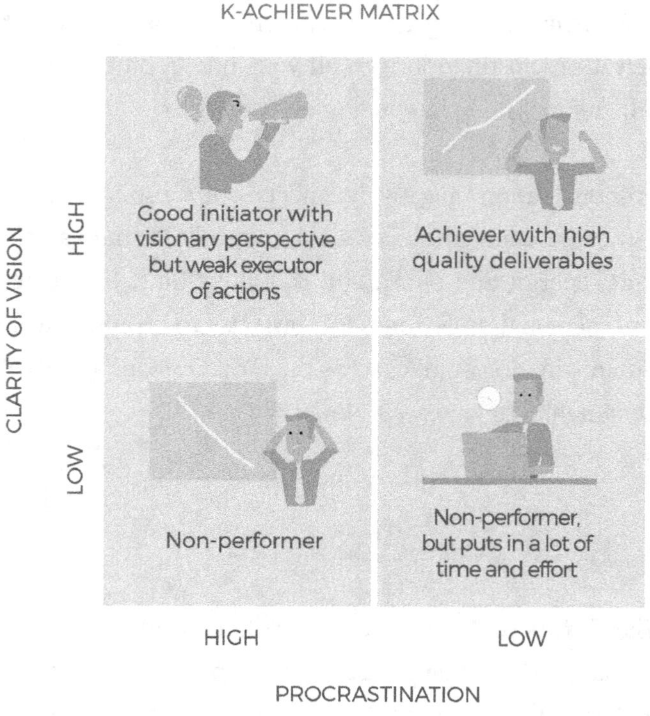

Figure 5.1 K-Achiever Matrix

Clarity of Vision	Procras- tination	Performance Category	Your Current Behavioural Status
High	Low	Achiever with high-quality deliverables	You possess the behavioural traits of a higher performer/ achiever who is advancing in the right direction.
High	High	Good initiator with visionary perspective but weak executor of actions	You tend to be a good initiator but are not able to follow up and complete deliverables as no appropriate action is taken despite clear goals being formulated.
Low	Low	Non- performer, but puts in a lot of effort and time	You are non- performing despite reasonable efforts, unable to achieve optimal outcomes or produce high-quality deliverables.

Low	High	Non-performer	You need help in setting and prioritising goals to assist in removing barriers to acting on tasks efficiently.

Table 5.1   K-Achiever Matrix analysis

Table 5.2 is a step-by-step guide on how to use the K-Achiever Matrix. To determine your current behavioural status in terms of clarity of vision and procrastination, evaluate yourself against these two elements. First, identify the quadrant that best resonates with you. Thereafter, determine your current performance category, which enables you to know your current behavioural status and allows you to be aware of the areas for improvement.

Steps	Action
1	Use the K-Achiever Matrix framework presented in Figure 5.1 to evaluate yourself against the two elements, namely clarity of vision and procrastination.
2	Identify yourself with one of the four quadrants (choose the best fit).
3	Identify your current behavioural status using Table 5.1, so that you become aware of the area(s) that you can improve in.

Table 5.2   How to use the K-Achiever Matrix

Once you have identified the root causes or reasons that led to procrastination, you can then mindfully address them in an organised manner. To deal with and overcome the issue on procrastination, we propose some simple yet effective strategies that you can adopt.

SIMPLE STRATEGIES TO OVERCOME PROCRASTINATION

1. Tighten the Deadline

Devise a tight deadline that propels you out of the procrastination state and gets you to do the work, by forcing you to view and perform your task creatively. Having a much-compressed time phase to finish off your task makes you potentially perform better, and makes you more effective and efficient. For example, if you have five weeks to complete a project, try to work out a schedule that enables you to finish it within four weeks so that you can start early and have more time for a review and a thorough checking and editing process, and even to have the work beefed up in terms of its rigour and quality. Adopt the idea of Parkinson's Law, which fundamentally requires you to put self-timed constraints on literally everything you do— even if there is no real need to do so. This self-imposed deadline will be the driving force or push factor to focus on your work instead of procrastinating.

2. Create a To-Do List

Devise a to-do list with checkboxes and stipulated deadlines beside each item. This enables you to monitor your tasks and work towards having the checkboxes ticked off diligently. The unchecked boxes are the actions to focus on. This helps you to keep a close track on your key tasks and serves as a continuous reminder to get things done without unnecessary delays, as the list gets added on to progressively.

In summary, the essence of this street-smart time mastery strategy is to first develop a crystal clear vision on what you want to achieve or who you want to become, and then overcome procrastination to immediately start taking significant and sustainable action on your vision. This is a quintessential skill of super achievers.

FIRST DEVELOP A CRYSTAL CLEAR VISION ON WHAT YOU WANT TO ACHIEVE.

Chapter 6

STRATEGY #2:
PRIORITISE YOUR PRIORITIES

*"Yesterday is gone. Tomorrow has not yet come.
We have only today. Let us begin."*

**- Mother Teresa,
nun and missionary**

20% of your activities account for
80% of your success, so give this
20% of tasks your highest priority.

ACTION STEP

Prioritise your tasks with absolute precision
and clarity.

 ## FOLLOW THE 80-20 RULE

In the 1900s, an Italian economist by the name of Pareto observed an unequal distribution of wealth in his country: that roughly 20% of the people owned 80% of the wealth. In the 1940s, this 80/20 Rule was named by quality management specialist Dr. Joseph Juran as the Pareto Principle. He also described it as the "vital few and trivial many".

The 80/20 Rule can be applied to any area of your life. For example, you may tend to wear 20% of your clothes 80% of the time. Some ladies we know own many bags but only use the same few bags most of the time. In business, 80% of a company's revenue is derived from 20% of its clients, and it's important to identify and build a strong relationship with this core group of high-paying clients. For students preparing for exams, 80% of what comes up in the exam is taken from 20% of the syllabus, so it is important to be familiar with the most important topics.

When applied to time mastery, the 80/20 Rule states that 80% of our results are due to 20% of our effort. In other words, 20% of the tasks you do will result in 80% of your success in goal achievement. Thus, it is important to prioritise your to-do list and identify what is critical to do first, so that you will not be caught up with the trivial stuff.

 ## ZERO IN ON THE HIGH-TICKET ITEMS

Always ask yourself, "What is the core 20% of study material that I should focus my efforts on, that will give me 80% of my results?"

> **FOCUS ON AND PRIORITISE ACTION ITEMS THAT ARE OF HIGH VALUE.**

Focus on and prioritise action items that are of high value. On a typical day, there may be numerous items that have piled up in your to-do list. Before you start on your tasks, take some time to have the tasks at hand prioritised. When you start to prioritise, identify the task that is of paramount importance in terms of meeting a deadline, and that would have the most positive impact on your studies and you as a student if you were to deal with it immediately. Resist the temptation to clear the not-so-vital, smaller tasks first. Always remind yourself to start with what is the most crucial.

 ## ESSENTIAL TIME-SAVER QUESTIONS

To guide you in evaluating which tasks to focus on as a priority, you can reflect on the following essential time-saver questions:

- Which task do I need to address first today to stand me in good stead tomorrow?

- Which task would get me into trouble or cause a negative effect if I do not get it done?

- What do my teacher, project group mates, or friends need most from me right now?

- Why is the top task I have identified the most important task that I have to do now?

 ## THE K-TIMESAVER MATRIX

The K-Timesaver Matrix is a tool that helps one to achieve optimal efficiency and effectiveness, by organising tasks into eight categories with clear and precise priorities. Figure 6.1 presents the K-Timesaver Matrix framework. It uses two primary variables, namely urgent and vital, to determine the priority of the task at hand. Urgent refers to tasks that need to be done immediately. However, the range of urgency can be varied, for example a task that falls under A1 is more urgent than one that falls under A2. Vital refers to tasks that are of importance but may not necessarily need to be done immediately. For example, a task that falls under B1 is more vital than one that falls under B2.

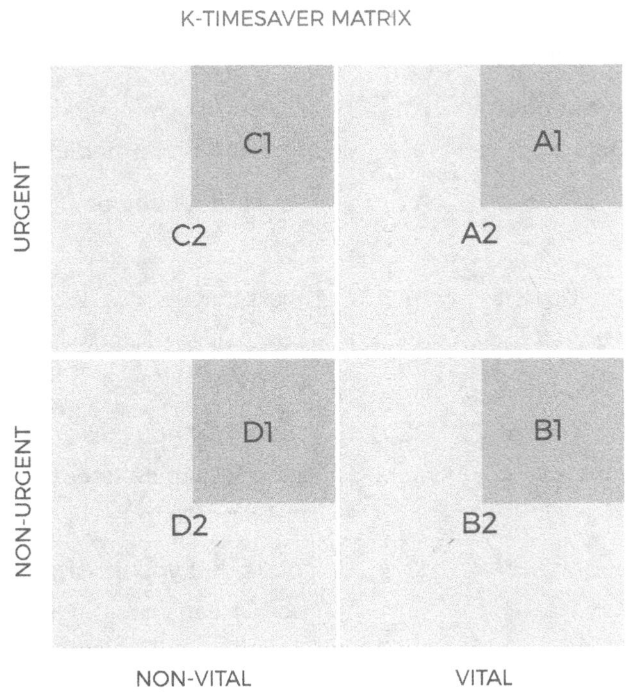

Figure 6.1 K-Timesaver Matrix

For every single task on your to-do list, use the following guidelines in Table 6.1 to determine its position in the K-Timesaver Matrix, based on on how urgent and how vital the task is.

Priority Categorisation	Symbol	Analysis
Urgent and Vital	A1	Tasks that you need to do first and do immediately
Urgent and Vital	A2	Tasks that you need to do first
Non-Urgent and Vital	B1	Tasks that you can do later but to be re-visited within a shorter duration
Non-Urgent and Vital	B2	Tasks that you can schedule to do later but to be re-visited
Urgent and Non-Vital	C1	Tasks that you need to do but can possibly be done through others via monitoring
Urgent and Non-Vital	C2	Tasks that you need to do but can possibly be done through empowering others

| Non-Urgent and Non-Vital | D1 | Tasks to be placed in the wish list and to be re-visited if time permits later |
| Non-Urgent and Non-Vital | D2 | Tasks to be removed completely |

Table 6.1   K-Timesaver Matrix analysis

Table 6.2 is a step-by-step guide on how to use the K-Timesaver Matrix. The first action is to draw up a laundry list of all the tasks that need to be addressed and dealt with. Next, use the K-Timesaver Matrix to evaluate how urgent and how vital each task is. Assign each of these tasks to one of the eight categories in the K-Timesaver Matrix and refer to the corresponding Analysis column in Table 6.1 for advice on how you should manage the task. This process enables you to not only organise the tasks in terms of priority but also get explicit guidance on what should be done.

Steps	Action
1	List down all the tasks that need to be addressed and dealt with.
2	Use the essential time-saver questions listed above to help you prioritise your tasks in terms of how urgent and how vital they are.
3	Assign each task to one of the eight categories in the K-Timesaver Matrix.
4	Refer to the corresponding Analysis column in Table 6.1 for advice on how you should manage each task.

Table 6.2   How to use the K-Timesaver Matrix

It is imperative for you to become proficient in prioritising your tasks and the best way to achieve this is via relentless practice. Many people struggle in having to prioritise multiple and varying tasks that require their attention. The ability to deal with such a situation requires you to be adept at organising what you need to do with absolute clarity. We trust the K-Timesaver Matrix will serve as an easy and user-friendly framework to guide you in completing your tasks effectively and efficiently.

In today's dynamic and fast-moving environment, you need to make quick and effective decisions to successfully navigate complex situations. Here, the bottom line is how well one can address the varying tasks in a systematic and expedient manner.

Chapter 7

STRATEGY #3:
FIND THE RIGHT TIME

"The time is always right to do what is right."

**- Martin Luther King, Jr.,
minister and civil rights activist**

High achievers do the right thing
at the right time, and avoid overcommitting
at the wrong time.

ACTION STEP

There is always a best time for doing anything.
Find the best time to work on your most
important tasks.

 HOW DO WE CHOOSE THE RIGHT TIME?

There is always a right time to do anything. When it comes to studying, we find it helpful to study the boring and heavy subjects at the times when we are most alert (which for us, is after dinner), and study the easier subjects when we feel more tired (usually after lunch).

> **THERE IS ALWAYS A RIGHT TIME TO DO ANYTHING.**

In order to have productive study sessions, it is important to strategically plan your revision schedule in such a way that you do the right task or study the right subject at the right time to match your energy levels. For instance, if you enjoy solving mathematics questions, then do them at "off-peak" periods when your energy levels are lower, so that you can still get through the task without falling asleep.

When it comes to exams, there is also a best time to answer certain questions. A common strategy used by top students is to first scan through the whole exam paper, and start by tackling the easiest questions or section to secure the easy marks. Leave the hardest questions to the last.

When it comes to working on a key priority that demands a lot of your mental resources, it is a good idea to work on it during the time blocks when you are most alert and energetic. For example, you may need to write a comprehensive project paper that is due in a month. If you are a morning person, then you should strategically carve out a time block in the early morning before you go to school or work, to work on the project paper. Go to bed at night an hour earlier and wake up in the morning an hour earlier if it works for you. On the other hand, if your energy levels are typically highest in the evening, say between 9pm to 11pm, then you should take full advantage of this strategic evening time block to work on your project. The ability to do the right thing at the right time is a hallmark trait of high achievers.

AVOID OVERCOMMITTING AT THE WRONG TIME

You must be pragmatic and realistic in agreeing to deliver commitments as your ability to deliver quality outcomes within the agreed-upon time frame reflects on your credibility. If the request comes at a bad time when your resources are severely stretched, you must develop the skill to say "No" with tact.

At times, you will be caught in an emotional dilemma, especially when the request comes from someone close. Nonetheless, it is important that you are truthful and do not make false commitments, which also shows that you respect the other person in ensuring their request is being fulfilled with your full commitment, resulting in quality deliverables. The inability to say "No" and fearing and worrying about what others will think will only result in high stress, especially when you are not able to complete the tasks in time.

For most of us, the act of saying "No" in a diplomatic and gracious manner does not come naturally. It is a crucial time-saving skill that can be developed, as you will learn in the following section.

Chapter 8

STRATEGY #4:
SAY "NO" TACTFULLY

"Focussing is about saying, "No"."

**- Steve Jobs,
co-founder of Apple Computer**

When you are overburdened, there are ways to decline the request and say "No" with tact, yet maintain a cordial and professional relationship with the other party.

> **ACTION STEP**
> Say "No" with tact and authenticity,
> earning respect from others, in order to
> avoid overcommitting and being unable
> to deliver your promised task with quality
> and efficiency.

 ## THE ART OF SAYING "NO"

There are two key reasons why saying "No" can be challenging. Firstly, it may disappoint, hurt, or anger the person, which is not something that can always be controlled. Secondly, you may need to continue working with the person, hence maintaining a good relationship becomes vital. Saying "No" in an incorrect manner can jeopardise the relationship.

Here are five essential strategies to master the art of saying "No" with tact as well as firmness and assertiveness:

1. Avoid Being Overly Nice

It is important to maintain diplomacy in our correspondences and dealings, but saying "Yes" all the time will result in you being overloaded, stressed, and burnt out. However, if you are upfront and honest about your priorities, requesters will understand and avoid approaching you unnecessarily in the future.

2.   Do Not Lie

Ensure you do not provide people with fake excuses as that is certainly not a good way to deal with the challenges at hand. Instead, be open and honest about why you are not able to support their requests right now.

3.   Provide a Reason with an Explanation

Take some time to explain your involvement and commitment regarding the important tasks currently taking up your time, and how taking on new tasks will highly affect the quality and timeliness of your deliverables. In a positive light, this only earns you respect as you will be perceived as an individual who is focussed on the quality of your commitment, and you will come across as authentic and trustworthy.

4.   Do Not Apologise Unnecessarily

People always start by saying, "I am sorry" to be polite, but actually, this only makes the correspondence much weaker. The point here is that you should be unapologetic and firm in guarding your precious time.

5.   Ask Them to Check Back Later

If you are keen on the opportunity but your plate is currently full, you may suggest that the requester check back with you at a later time. For example, you can reply, "This sounds like an interesting opportunity; however, I cannot commit at this juncture. Perhaps you could check back with me [give a time frame]."

> YOU SHOULD BE UNAPOLOGETIC AND FIRM IN GUARDING YOUR PRECIOUS TIME.

The art of saying "No" tactfully is a competency that is mastered by high achievers. It allows you to be aware of your own commitments, be honest and fair to yourself in terms of personal well-being, and not be unintentionally overwhelmed by obligatory commitments. To be clear, we are not proposing that you say "No" to every single task and request that comes your way, as you need to know when to say "Yes" to important priorities. The key is to strike a fine balance between behaving assertively and maintaining diplomacy and a cordial relationship with the people around you.

Chapter 9

STRATEGY #5: MAINTAIN A LASER FOCUS

*"Concentrate all your thoughts upon
the work at hand. The sun's rays do not burn
until brought to a focus."*

**- Alexander Graham Bell,
scientist and inventor**

For maximum efficiency,
one must fully focus on the task at hand
and limit multitasking.

ACTION STEP

Focus 100% on a single task
at any one time.

THE SIGNIFICANCE OF DEVELOPING A LASER FOCUS

Ever wondered what is the true meaning of the term "laser focus"? A laser is a device that emits high-intensity light of a single wavelength that is accurately focussed into a narrow, high-energy beam. When you are focussing like a laser, it effectively means you are directing your entire attention and all of your energy on the task in front of you. That translates to single-tasking, which is the recommended approach for high achievement.

Multitasking, on the other hand, refers to performing or getting involved in various tasks concurrently. It is a commonly-held belief that we can multitask and do multiple tasks effectively at the same time. However, the evidence shows that we are not able to effectively focus on more than one thing at any one time. Even if we can complete the tasks, the question is whether the quality of the completed tasks is good enough. Hence, it is highly advisable to focus and concentrate on one thing and aim to achieve higher productivity and quality outcomes.

We are not completely against multitasking, because it can be a valuable time saver if you know how to use it to your advantage. We personally find it useful to multitask

> **MULTITASK UNIMPORTANT ACTIVITIES SO THAT YOU DO NOT END UP SPENDING TOO MUCH TIME ON THEM.**

unimportant activities so that we do not end up spending too much time on them. However, for your most important, major tasks that fall within the top 20% of your priorities, such as your homework and revision for exams, you will benefit more from concentrating fully than from multitasking.

When you are studying, focus your entire energy and attention on the subject matter. One trick that we find useful is to visualise ourselves as being in an empty tunnel, seeing nothing but what is in front of us. Before you begin a study session, it is a good practice to clear your desk, close all chat windows, turn off message notifications on your electronic devices, and log off from Facebook or other social networks. As your mobile phone is likely to be a major source of distraction, you may want to put it further away from your desk. For example, you can place your mobile phone in a small storage container at least two metres away from where you are sitting, so that you cannot conveniently reach out for it. By doing so, you minimise disruptive distractions so that you can remain fully focussed on the task at hand.

The first step in overcoming or limiting multitasking is to comprehend the root causes and motivations that led to it. Once you can identify and are aware of the contributing factors, you can then take the appropriate actions to remedy them. We have examined the common underlying reasons that lead to multitasking and propose the following strategies that will empower you to focus on single-tasking, so that you can achieve higher quality outcomes with increased efficiency.

 ## STRATEGIES TO LIMIT MULTITASKING

1. Prioritised To-Do List

Devise and adopt the use of to-do lists. In your list, you could group action items in three categories, namely urgent (immediate), important (prioritise first), and to be done within a certain time frame (i.e., within a week or within a month).

2. Time Blocks

Plan the day in blocks that are tagged with time periods; for example, setting aside the first two to three hours of the early morning to address urgent matters. Set aside specific time-slots to address and reply emails, return phone calls, attend project meetings, perform school-related assignments, and revise your work. Cater some time for strategic planning and analysis of how you can further improve the use of your time.

3.   Self-Awareness Check

If you find yourself back to doing tasks concurrently, stop, take a short break, re-prioritise, and then proceed to focus on the tasks on hand.

To achieve high quality and effective outcomes, you must devote your fullest attention and energy to work on your task till completion, or till you reach a significant milestone for a big project. The trait of being highly focussed can be cultivated by regularly applying the practical strategies to restrict multitasking as we have discussed in this chapter. Being focussed may sound simple, but when we are confronted with multiple tasks that demand our attention at the same time, it is very easy to fall back into the trap of multitasking. The act of being fully focussed on a single task reaps numerous positive benefits in terms of elevating the quality of your work or study, and super-charging your productivity.

Chapter 10

STRATEGY #6:
RIDE ON MOMENTUM

*"You don't have to be great to start,
but you have to start to be great."*

**- Zig Ziglar,
motivational speaker**

It is difficult to move when you are at rest.
It is difficult to stop when you are moving fast.

ACTION STEP

1. Start doing the task for one minute.
2. Don't stop until you finish the task.
3. Minimise and work around interruptions.

 **THE LAW OF MOMENTUM**

Newton's first law of motion states that an object at rest will continue to remain at rest unless an external force acts on it, and a moving object will continue to move until an external force acts on it.

To a large extent, our lives are governed by this law. What this basically means for us is that it is difficult to start something, but once it is started, it is difficult to stop. To illustrate this law, let us look at some real-life scenarios. When you ride a bicycle, pedalling to get the bicycle moving at the start takes disproportionately more effort than subsequent pedalling, when the bicycle is already in motion. The hardest part of going out for a jog to improve your fitness is first getting changed into running gear and stepping out of the house, particularly when you are in a comfortable and relaxed state at home. Once you start jogging, it is easy to continue as long as your level of fitness permits.

> **IT IS DIFFICULT TO START SOMETHING, BUT ONCE IT IS STARTED, IT IS DIFFICULT TO STOP.**

When we were students, we usually found it very tough to begin writing a new essay or article. We found ourselves coming up with all sorts of excuses: "The weather is bad." "I need a break. "I have more important things to do now." "I am too tired." "I will write tomorrow." There was always some excuse to delay writing. However, once we started writing the first paragraph, we found it much easier to complete the rest of the article. That is the beauty of Newton's first law.

THE ONE-MINUTE STRATEGY

We use the One-Minute Strategy to overcome the initial inertia. It works like this: The next time you procrastinate when faced with a monumental task, say for example, doing a difficult assignment, simply tell yourself that you're going to sit down and do it for one minute, then after that you can relax and do whatever you want. This works because once you start, the law of momentum dictates that you will find it more difficult to stop when you are in the thick of the action. Therefore, it is likely that you will finish doing the whole assignment, or if not, complete a significant chunk of it.

WORK AROUND INTERRUPTIONS

The level of your personal effectiveness in getting tasks at hand done depends on how much uninterrupted time you get in the day to work on important tasks. It is important to acknowledge and explicitly identify the distractions that tend to disrupt your studies or tasks, then find a solution to work around them.

To effectively deal with and work around the interruptions, it is vital for you to identify the contributing causes behind them. We have identified the common reasons for these interruptions and propose strategies to work around them.

1.   **Focus Single-Mindedly on the Task**

The key in managing time well is not to get distracted. For example, avoid replying to WhatsApp messages, answering phone calls, and checking emails when you are studying, revising, doing homework, or in the middle of doing something important. Once you have broken your momentum, it can be tough to re-establish it. Instead, focus 100% on the task at hand till it is successfully completed.

2.   **Adopt the Pomodoro Technique**

The Pomodoro technique is a time management approach invented by Francesro Cirillo in the late 1980s. This approach focusses on using planned intervals to facilitate regular breaks and lessen the impact of internal and external interruptions. Firstly, you begin by deciding on the task to tackle. Then, for 25 minutes, you focus completely on the task, followed by taking a five-minute break where you remove yourself from work. This qualifies as one set. This cycle is to be repeated till the task is completed. It is also advisable to take a longer break of 15 to 25 minutes after 3 to 4 hours of work, and the routine to be repeated.

For example, imagine you are preparing for an examination. Firstly, you block off a stipulated number of hours, ensuring there are no interruptions. You allocate two hours of continuous revision where you fully focus on it. Thereafter, you take a 10-15-minute break to relax and unwind. This qualifies as one set. Depending on the total time that you have allocated for revision that day, you can repeat the routine to fit your planned schedule.

Leveraging on momentum is so powerful that you will be able to achieve much more than what you think you can do. We have illustrated how the One-Minute Strategy can kickstart you into taking immediate action, and shared practical tips to work around the potential interruptions that can hinder the flow of your momentum. By using momentum in your favour, you can easily overcome the initial inertia to start your work or study. Thereafter, you will naturally enter a state of flow that empowers you to swiftly complete the rest of the task.

CONCLUDING THOUGHTS

"Time = Life; therefore, waste your time and waste your life, or master your time and master your life."

**- Alan Lakein,
author of *How to Get Control of Your Time and Your Life***

Finally, the key question that you need to ask yourself is, "Am I in control of my time and able to perform my tasks productively?" This book's goal is to provide you with practical and easy-to-use tools to manage your time effectively so you can take back control of your daily life.

Time mastery is the cornerstone skill that enables you to:

1.   Enhance personal efficiency and effectiveness

2.   Improve study and work productivity

3.   Set crystal clear priorities and high-value goals

4.   Create more quality time that contributes to work-life harmony

5.   Develop good values and habits

6.   Avoid any health issues and burn-out

We hope that the pragmatic strategies and tips shared in this book will enable you to optimise your time, prioritise your tasks, eliminate distractions, and overcome procrastination, and leave you with higher quality time to do more. For further reading on strategies for time mastery, visit timemasterylab.com.

In summary, if you organise your time well by avoiding time traps, eliminating time wasters, and making full use of the 6 street-smart strategies of time mastery, you will be more productive in your daily life and in your studies. As a result, you can free up more precious time for yourself and your family, have more time to rest and recharge, and ultimately be happier.

To conclude, we leave you with this nugget of timeless wisdom on personal time mastery that has served us very well over the years:

DO THE RIGHT THINGS FIRST AND DO THEM FAST.

DR. EUGENE SERN-TING TAN is a Dermatologist at the National Skin Centre. He graduated from the National University of Singapore in 2006. After completing his broad-based dermatology training at the National Skin Centre, he underwent advanced subspecialty training in photodermatology, psoriasis, and paediatric dermatology at St. John's Institute of Dermatology at Guy's and St. Thomas' Hospitals in London under the Health Manpower Development Programme (HMDP). Over the years, Dr. Tan has published over 30 research articles in regional and international scientific journals. He has co-authored two books, namely *Love Clinic – How To Lose Your Bachelor's Degree* and *Phototherapy and Photodiagnostic Methods for the Practitioner*, as well as contributed chapters to several books on dermatology. He volunteers as an ad-hoc reviewer for several medical journals, and is currently the Chief Editor of the *Journal of Business, Sciences, and Technology*. As an invited speaker, Dr. Tan has delivered numerous talks at various local and regional conferences. He is actively committed to teaching, with appointed educational roles in all three local medical schools in Singapore. Dr. Tan has a keen interest in personal development and believes that time mastery is an essential skill for anyone who desires greater achievement and happiness in life.

DR. KUMARAN RAJARAM has over 18 years of corporate leadership and senior management experience in organisational development and strategic and change management. He has served as the Head and the Director of Academic Affairs and Business Development for Asia Pacific, and thereafter, as the CEO of a global leadership and organisational learning consulting firm before he became a researcher and educator. Dr. Rajaram has a Ph.D. with Distinction in Business and Management, majoring in Organisational Learning Science. He is a Senior Lecturer and Course Chair at Nanyang Business School and a Research Fellow-Affiliate with the Centre for Research and Development in Learning. He is an expert in the field of leadership, management education, learning culture, and innovation where he was instrumental in transforming and implementing flipped-classroom pedagogy and team-based learning in the course he chairs. He has received multiple competitive school-, university-, and national-level research grants and awards. He has published in management education, learning culture in a multi-disciplinary context, and internationalisation of business education. Dr. Rajaram is also the Founder of the Research Lab for Learning Innovations and Culture of Learning – InnovsolvLearn, Creative Solutions (InnosolvLearn.com). He believes that time mastery is a vital skill for those who aspire to attain greater accomplishment and happiness in life.

www.ingramcontent.com/pod-product-compliance
Lightning Source LLC
Chambersburg PA
CBHW061246140726
47998CB00006B/2112